The God of Every Moment

VERSES FOR THE SOUL'S JOURNEY

BADARIAKOR LANGSTIEH

BlueRose ONE.com
Stories Matter
NewDelhi • London

BLUEROSE PUBLISHERS
India | U.K.

BlueRoseONE.com
Stories Matter
NewDelhi • London

For permissions requests or inquiries regarding this publication, please contact:

BLUEROSE PUBLISHERS
www.BlueRoseONE.com
info@bluerosepublishers.com
+91 8882 898 898
+4407342408967

ISBN: 978-93-7542-368-3

Cover design: Aafiya Saifi
Typesetting: Namrata Saini

First Edition: March 2026

FIVE VERSES FROM THE BIBLE.

- ***PSALM-73:26***
  "My flesh and my Heart may fail, but God is the strength of my Heart and my portion forever".

- ***EXODUS-14:14***
  "The Lord will fight for you; you need only to be still".

- ***JAMES-1:5***
  "If any of you lacks Wisdom, you should ask God, who gives generously to all without finding fault, and it will be given to you".

- ***PROVERBS-3:5-6***
  "Trust in the Lord with all your Heart and lean not on your own understanding; in all ways submit to Him, and He will make your paths straight".

- ***2 TIMOTHY-1:7***
  "God has not given us a spirit of fear, but of Power and of Love and of a sound mind".

(I)

A Mother's prayer, a whisper sigh,
Lifts her child up to the morning sky,
With tears and hope, she prays with glee,
For protection, guidance, a Mother's **plea.**

In every test, she's there to cheer,
Her Love and Faith, dispel all fears,
With every breath, she whispers low,
"Keep my Child safe, as they grow".

Through trials and tribulations, she's **Strong,**
Her Prayers ascend, all day long.
A Mother's heart, beats with Love and pain,
Her Prayer is pure, her Love remains.

In quiet moments, she bows her head,
Giving thanks, for life ahead.
Her heart beats fast, with Love so bright,
A Mother's prayer, a guiding light.

With arms outstretched, she waits with cheer,
For her child's dreams, to soon appear.
A Mother's prayer, a work of art,
A Love that's pure, straight from the Heart.

A Mother's prayer, a treasure rare,
A Love that's strong, beyond compare.
It echoes through, the years and time,
A Mother's prayer, forever divine.

(II)

Late nights and dark circles too,
A **price** paid for dreams anew.
Hard work and dedication shine,
Silent **tears** and **struggles** divine.

God sees it all, every single night,
Every Sacrifice, every desperate fight.
He **answers** prayers in **His** perfect time,
Bringing forth success, a **wondrous** rhyme.

Tears of struggle turn to joy and pride,
As hard work pays off, and dreams abide.
So hold on tight, don't lose your way,
God's timing is perfect, come what may.

Keep pushing forward, through the darkest night,
Your breakthrough is coming, shining bright.
Your silent tears, your hard-won fight,
Will be worth it all, in God's perfect light.

(III)

... Since ancient times, no ear has heard,
No eyes has seen a God like you, Lord,
Your work wonders for those who wait,
Rewarding faith with Grace so great.
You meet the righteous with delight,
Those who remembers your ways in might,
Your mercies shines like morning light,
Guiding those who trust in your greatest might.

(IV)

My God is still good, through every test,
In turmoil's fire, He's always best.
When darkness falls, and fears arise,
His faithfulness shines, like morning skies.

Through stormy nights and troubled seas,
He's my Anchor, my peace, my breeze,
When doubts creep in, and worries roam,
His Love remains, my Heart's safe home.

In every trial, He's my guide,
My Strength, My Comfort, My Pride.
When all seems lost, and I'm astray,
He leads me forward, come what may.

With every step, He's by my side,
My Rock, My Saviour, My Constant guide,
In His presence, I am not alone,
He walks with me, wherever I may roam.

My God is still good, through it all,
Forever Faithful, standing tall,
His Love endures, through every pain,
A Love that's constant, forever the same.

- ***<u>ISAIAH-40:31</u>***

  "But those who Hope in the Lord, will renew their strength. They will soar on wings like Eagles; they will run and not grow weary, they will walk and not be faint".

(V)

Lord, be my anchor when I'm weak and worn,
Be my Comforter, when life's storms rage on,
In times of doubt, be my guiding light,
And when I'm lost, lead me through the dark.
Be my Strength when fears and worries creep,
And when I'm broken, be my Soul's repair,
In your presence, let me find my peace,
And with your Love, let my Heart release.

(VI)

With open arms, God's love enfolds me deep,
A shelter from life's storms, where I can sleep,
In every moment, Love's presence I feel,
A Constant Guide, through trials I reveal.
With gentle whispers, God's heart speaks to mine,
A love that's pure, and forever divine;
In his eyes, I'm cherished, loved and free,
Forever held, in God's love, I'm me.

- ***JEREMIAH-17:7-8***

  "But blessed is the one who trust in the Lord, whose confidence is in Him. They will be like a tree planted by the water that sends out its roots by the stream. It doesn't fear when heat comes; its leaves are always green. It has no worries in a year of drought and never fails to bear fruits".

(VII)

In your hands, my story's written page,
Guided by Faith, I'll follow your stage,
With every step, your Love I'll engage;
Trusting your plans, through life's joys and rage.
You see the path, through trials and strife,
Leading me forward, to a brighter life.
In your goodness, my heart finds its place,
Forever with you, I'll walk in your Grace.

(VIII)

Teach them well, dear parents, guide them right,
Care for their hearts, and shine with all your might,
Innocence abounds, in their youthful eyes,
Protect it dearly, from life's disguise.

Social media's sway, a subtle creep,
Smartphones' glow, a constant seep,
Into their minds, a world untamed,
Guard them wisely, or innocence will wane.

Teach them values, moral strong and true,
Help them discern, what's right and what to do,
Care for their souls, and nurture their dreams,
And keep their hearts, from life's extremes.

In this digital age, be vigilant and wise,
Set boundaries firm, and open eyes,
To the world's vastness, and its hidden source,
Guide them gently, with Love and care.

For childhood's fleeting, and innocence rare,
Treasure these moments, beyond compare,
Teach, care, and protect with all your might,
And give your children, a guiding light.

- ***<u>PROVERBS-22:6</u>***

  "Train up a child in the way he should go, and when he is old he will not depart from it".

(IX)

Oh, gentle soul, who find solace deep,
In quiet hours, where thoughts softly creep.
The world outside, with all its din,
Fades into calm, as peace draws within.
In solitude, you find your way,
A world of thoughts, a universe to roam;
In silence, you find your peaceful home.
May your solitude be truly blessed,
For in the stillness, you find your voice,
A gentle whisper, a heartfelt choice.

- ***ISAIAH-30:15***

  *"In quietness and trust is your **STRENGTH**".*

(X)

In city's labyrinthine streets I stray,
A thousand thoughts, my constant sway;
The world outside recedes from view,
As inner dialogues my soul pursue.
The city's pulse, a distant hum,
My heart beats slow, my thought become
A symphony of introspection deep,
In solitude, my spirit finds its keep.

(XI)

Those we love never truly die,
Their memory stays forever nigh,
Though we can't see them with our eyes,
Their presence remains, a heartfelt surprise.

In every breeze, we feel their sigh,
In every sunbeam, their loving light,
Their whisper echo, a gentle, guiding light,
A comforting feeling, that they're still in sight.

Their love remains, a flame that burns bright,
A beacon in darkness, a guiding light,
Though they may be gone, their memory stays near,
A bittersweet reminder, of the Love we hold dear.

Let us cherish, the memories we share,
And hold them close, with a loving care
For though they may be gone, their love remains,
A constant presence, that forever sustains.

(XII)

An iron sharpens iron's edge,
A friend sharpens a friend's pledge,
Together they grow, side by side,
Refining each other, with love as their guide.

Through laughter and tears, they stand as one,
Sharpening each other, till the day is done,
Their bond grows stronger, their hearts more bright,
A friendship like iron, sharpened with delight.

With every test, their trust takes hold,
Their friendship deepens, young and old,
Through thick and thin, they stand as one,
A sharpened bond, forever won.

So let us cherish friendships true,
That sharpen us, and see us through,
For in their Love, we find our way,
And together we shine, come what may.

- ***<u>PROVERBS-17:17</u>***

  "A friend loves at all times, and a brother is born for a time of adversity".

(XIII)

Why Stars?

Because I adore them, twinkling bright,
A canvas of diamonds, in the velvet night,
Their gentle sparkle, a reflection of His face,
A reminder of God's glory, in every time and place.

Their celestial music, a symphony so fine,
Echoes of the heavens, a harmony divine,
Their light dances across, the expanse of Space,
A celestial showcase, of God's wondrous grace.

In the stillness of night, I gaze upon their glow,
And I am reminded of God's love that shines so bright,
A love that guides me, through life's joys and fears,
A love that's constant, through all my doubts and tears.

So I'll keep looking up at the starry sky,
And I'll remember God's glory, as it passes me by,
For in the beauty of stars, I see a glimpse of His face,
A reflection of God's glory, in every time and place.

- ***<u>PSALM-147:4</u>***
  "He counts the stars and calls them all by name."

(XIV)

I am a poet, silent and still,
My words run deep, like an unspoken will.
I know the power of language and art,
A careless phrase can tear the heart.

In silence, I find my voice,
A quiet reflection, a heartfelt choice,
To speak or not, a poet's dilemma stands,
Lest words, like autumn leaves, wither in the hands.

The depth of words, a labyrinth to explore,
A maze of meaning, where emotions roar,
I weigh each word, like a precious stone,
Lest it betray the silence I call home.

So let me be still, and let the words descend,
Like a gentle rain, that nourishes and mends,
For in the silence, I found my poetic voice,
A whispered promise, a heartfelt, poignant choice.

(XV)

In the stillness, I wait for your hand,
To move, to guide, to make your plan,
Unfold before me like a work of art,
A **Masterpiece**, crafted with Love in your heart.

Your timing is perfect, a symphony so fine,
A dance of moments, intertwined with divine,
You weave the thread of my life into a tapestry so grand,
A story of **Redemption** written by your hand.

I've learned to trust in your **Sovereign** might,
To wait patiently, for your perfect light,
To shine upon my path and guide me on my way,
To trust that your timing , is always perfect every day.

In your perfect timing, I find peace and rest,
A sense of calm, that the World cannot possess,
A **Confidence** that you are always in control,
A **Faith** that your timing is always perfect and whole.

So I'll wait on you, Lord, and trust in your **plans,**
Knowing that your timing is always perfect,
and always in your hand.

- ***<u>ECCLESIASTES-3:11</u>***
  *"He has made everything **BEAUTIFUL** in His time."*

(XVI)

To the **Dreamers,** the **Believers,** the **Heart** that beats strong,
To the one who's searching, seeking and holding on,
To the soul that's weary, worn and torn apart,
Know that you're seen, heard and loved from the very start.

You are a **Universe** of possibility, a cosmos of might,
A shining star that sparkles with beauty and light,
Your worth is not measured by the opinions of others,
You are enough, just as you are, in this moment, forever.

To the one who's struggling, who's lost and alone,
Know that you are not forgotten, you are not unknown,
You are a precious thread in the intricate tapestry of life,
Connected to every soul, every heart, every strife.

You are strong, resilient and capable of greatness,
A warrior who's fought battles and emerged
with scars and greatness.
Your voice matters, your story counts, your life has purpose,
Don't let anyone dull your sparkle, or silence your voice.

To whom it may concern know that you are loved,
You are valued, you are cherished, from above,
You're a precious gem, a unique work of art,
A Masterpiece, crafted with Love and placed in the Heart.

So hold your head high, let your spirit roar,
Remember that you are loved, you are enough, forevermore,
To whom it may concern, know that you are not alone,
You're a part of the community, a family that's **Home.**

- ***<u>EPHESIANS-2:10</u>***

  "You are God's Masterpiece."

(XVII)

In my weakness, I come to you,
My Lord, My Saviour, my heart anew,
I'm frail and fragile, prone to stray,
But your grace, oh God, is sufficient each day.

When trials rage like a stormy sea,
And doubts assail, and fears torment me,
I cling to your promise, dear and true,
"Your Grace is sufficient for me."

In the darkness, your light shines bright,
Guiding me through life's plodding night,
Your Strength is made perfect in my weakness,
Helping me stand, though I stumble and falter in sickness.

So I'll boast in my frailty, yes, I'll boast,
For in my weakness, your power is toasted,
Your grace, oh God, is all I need,
Sufficient for me, indeed!

May your grace, dear Lord, be my heart's refrain,
My Soul's solace, my life's sustaining strain,
For your grace, oh God, is sufficient for me,
Now and forever, I'll trust in your mercy.

- ***2 CORINTHIANS-12:9***
  "Your **GRACE** *is sufficient for me."*

(XVIII)

My help comes from the one who reigns,
Creator of Heaven, Earth and all domains,
The Maker of the Stars that shines so bright,
The one who holds my life, day and night.

When fears and doubts assail my soul,
And darkness closes in, making me lose control,
I lift my eyes to Heaven's throne,
And remember that my help comes from the one who's known.

The mountains may shake, the Earth may sway,
But My Rock, My God, remains steadfast each day,
He watches over me, guiding my way,
And fills my heart with peace, come what may.

My help comes from the Lord, the Creator true,
The one who formed the Heavens and the Earth anew,
I trust in Him, my heart at rest,
For my help comes from the one who loves me best.

(XIX)

In the chaos, He whispers low,
"Be **Still,** dear Heart, and know",
That I am your God, your Rock, your Guide,
Your shelter in life's turbulent tide.

When fears and doubts assail your mind,
And darkness closes in, be **Still** and find,
My presence in the quiet, peaceful place,
Where Love and Trust dispel the darkest **space.**

Let go of worries, let go of fears,
And in the Stillness, dry your tears,
For I am with you, always near,
Your God, your Saviour, your Heart's dear.

Be **still,** dear one, and know I'm yours,
Your faithful God, who calms life's roar,
In my presence, find your peaceful nest,
And know that **I AM YOUR GOD, I KNOW BEST!**

(XX)

In the depths of questioning and doubt,
Where fears and uncertainties shout,
I search for answers, night and day,
But in the silence, I hear Him say,

"Beyond the **Why** and **Why not, I AM",**
A gentle whisper that calms the storm within,
A reminder of His presence, always be near,
A love that's constant, dispelling every fear.

In the darkness, He is my guiding light,
A beacon of **Hope,** shining through the night,
When reasons falter, and understanding fails,
His Love remains, an **anchor** that never fails.

Beyond the **Why** and **Why not,** I'll trust,
In the goodness of my Saviour Jesus,
In His Mercy, I'll find peace and rest,
And in His Love, my Heart will be Blessed.

(XXI)

In the vastness of the midnight sky,
A canvas of diamonds, twinkling high,
I gaze upon the shooting stars up bright,
A celestial showcase, a breath-taking sight.

Their fleeting paths, a moment's glance,
A spark of beauty, a cosmic dance,
Like my life's journey, brief and fast,
A moment's shine, within the vast.

And yet, in this grand tapestry so fine,
I am not just a thread, but a divine design,
For in the beauty of these stars above,
I see the hand of God; an unconditional love.

How great is our God, who paints the sky,
With colours bright, and a gentle sigh,
Who whispers secrets, in the stars' soft light,
And fills my heart, with wonder and delight.

In the shooting stars, I see His hand,
A Masterpiece of Love, in this celestial land,
A reminder of his presence, always near,
A guiding light, that calms my deepest fears.

Me and shooting stars, a moment's pause,
A reflection of God's love, in the cosmic cause,
A dance of wonders, in the starry night,
A celebration of His greatness, a pure delight.

- ***JAMES-1:17***

  _"Every good gift and every perfect gift is from above, coming down from the Father of Lights, with whom there is no variation or shadow due to change."

(XXII)

To all the people dear to me;
You're the Sunshine that brightens my day,
The calm in every stormy way,
Your love and support, a guiding light,
Help me migrate through life's plodding night.

Your smile a treasure to behold,
A precious gift that never grows old,
Your laughter, music to my ears,
A joy that banishes all doubts and fears.

In times of joy, you celebrate with me,
In times of sorrow, you comfort and set me free,
You're My Rock, my shelter and my friend,
Together, our bond will never end.

So here's to you, dear ones, a thank you from the heart,
For being there, for never departing,
I cherish every moment we share,
And look forward to many more memories to spare.

(XXIII)

A gentle ear, a caring soul,
A listener's heart, makes us whole,
In a World of noise and busy pace,
A listener's calm, brings a peaceful space.

With attentive eyes, and an open mind,
A good listener, leaves hearts and souls aligned,
They hear the words, the tone, the sigh,
And in the silence, a deeper truth comes nigh.

Their presence is a gift, a treasure rare,
A safe haven, where hearts can share,
No judgement, no advice, just a listening ear,
A good listener, wipes away each tear.

So let us cherish these gentle souls,
Who listens with Love, and makes our hearts whole,
For in their listening, we find a peaceful nest,
A place to rest, and be our true best.

(XXIV)

In times of trouble, when my heart is weak,
I call on Jesus, my soul to seek,
He lifts me up, on eagle's wings,
And carries me, through life's turbulent springs,

When darkness falls, and fears arise,
He whispers peace, and opens weary eyes,
His presence calms my anxious soul,
And in His arms, I am made whole.

Like a Shepherd, He guides me along,
Through valleys' low and mountains' strong,
He carries me, when I'm too weak,
And in His love, my heart find a retreat.

So I'll trust in Him, through every test,
And let the Lord, carry me to my best,
For in His care, I am safe and sound,
And with Him, I'll walk on holy ground.

ROMANS-9:20-21

"But who are you, a human being, to talk back to God? Shall what is formed say to the one who formed it, 'Why did you make me like this?'. Does not the Potter have the right to make out of the same lump of clay some pottery for special purposes and some for common use?".

(XXV)

In the sky, a wondrous sight,
A rainbow stretches, vibrant and bright,
A symbol of Hope, a promise so true,
A reminder of God's love, shining through.

With colours so bold, and hues so divine,
The Rainbow proclaims, God's creative design,
Red, Orange, Violet, Indigo, Yellow, Green and Blue,
A Masterpiece of Beauty, for me and you.

After the rain and storm, the rainbow appears,
A sign of God's covenant, through all our fears,
A promise of protection, a love that's so strong,
A reminder that God is always with us, all day long.

So let us marvel at this wondrous sight,
And give thanks to God, for His creation so bright,
May the rainbow remind us of God's love and care,
And fills our hearts with joy, and our spirits with prayer.

(XXVI)

Visit many good books, but live in the Bible,
For in its pages, wisdom and truth enable,
Other books may inform, educate and delight,
But the Bible's words bring life and shine with divine light.

In its sacred texts, find solace, peace and rest,
Guidance for life's journey and a heavenly quest,
The Bible's stories, poems and proverbs too,
Offer timeless wisdom and a love that's forever true.

So visit many good books, but make the Bible your Home,
Where God's love and wisdom awaits and forever known,
For in its words, you'll find life, hope and a peaceful heart,
A treasure trove of spiritual wealth, that will never depart.

MATTHEW-19:14

"Let the little children come to me, and do not hinder them, for the Kingdom of Heaven belongs to such as these."

(XXVII)

Softly shines the morning sun,
Reflecting innocence, just begun,
A child's laughter echoes free,
Unbridled joy, wild and carefree.

Tiny hands, pure heart of gold,
Unwritten pages, stories untold,
Curious eyes, full of wonders wide,
Sparkling in life, side by side.

Smiles abound, tears fall like rain,
Emotions raw, no hidden pain,
Giggles echo, contagious delight,
Spontaneous hugs, warm and bright.

Innocence radiates, a beacon light,
Unmarred by Worldly sight,
Trustful eyes, open wide with glee,
A reflection of pure humanity.

Little one, cherish this precious stage,
Unspoiled and free, turn life's page,
May laughter echo, tears dry fast,
Forever preserve your innocent heart at last.

(XXVIII)

Small fingers, tiny voice, a smile so wide,
A compliment from innocent eyes, my heart inside,
Your words, a sunshine ray, brighten up my day,
A child's sincerity, never fades away.

"Your hair looks pretty", or "I like your tie",
Simple phrases, yet heartfelt, reaching the sky,
Unfiltered kindness, pure and true,
A gift from little ones, shining through.

Their eyes sparkle, as they speak from the heart,
No hidden agendas, just love's pure start,
Innocence abounds, in every single line,
A child's compliment, forever divine.

May we retain, this genuine charm,
Embracing kindness, dispelling alarms,
For in little hands, and tiny voices too,
Lies a World of Love, shining pure and true.

(XXIX)

In darkness, you shone as my guiding light,
My Saviour, My Healer, banishing endless night,
Through life's turmoil, your sacrifice set me free,
By your blood, my wounds healed, restored to be.

Your eternal love aligned each chapter's might,
Weaving moments, seconds, into eternal delight,
Faithful through eternity, forever true,
Gratitude overflows, for all you've accomplished anew.

New pages unfold, as your story unfolds,
A tapestry rich, with promises yet untold,
In awe, I praise, your majesty divine,
Forever grateful, heart and soul entwine.

Your presence illuminate life's plodding way,
A beacon shining bright, night's darkest day,
My heart beats for you, my Soul sings your praise,
Eternal devotion, in joyous, loving ways.

In your footsteps, I walk, hand in hand,
Through trials and triumphs, in your promised land,
My testimony echoes, a heartfelt refrain,
You, LORD, My Saviour, My Healer, forever sustain.

(XXX)

The Lord cares for you, through every test,
Guiding and protecting, always best,
In trials and storms, He's your peaceful shore,
Comforting and strengthening, forevermore.

His love surrounds you, like mountains high,
Shielding from harm, with a watchful eye,
Through life's darkest valleys, He walks beside,
Illuminating paths, with gentle stride.

The Lord's compassion, heals heart's deep pain,
Soothing fears, calming life's turbulent rain,
His gentle whispers, reassure your soul,
"You are loved, cherished, made whole".

In weary moments, when strength fades away,
He lifts and carries, come what may,
Through every struggle, He stands as your might,
Empowering resilience, shining his light.

Trust in his goodness, rest in his care,
The Lord's loving heart, forever aware,
Your life, a treasure, precious in His sight,
The Lord cares for you, day and endless night.

(XXXI)

Life's fleeting breath, like flowers that bloom,
Clouds drifting by, vapours dissolving soon,
Our Creator hold our lifespan's gentle thread,
Assigning us purpose, a mission to be said.

We journey on, with Hearts that beat for Him,
Vessels of Love, carrying His will within,
Our Earthly stay, a temporary, sacred trust,
Fulfilling His plan, with each faithful dust.

Jesus prepares our Heavenly Home,
Where love and joy forever roam,
Our hearts' desire, to please HIM each day,
Embracing His will, come what may.

With every breath, we'll serve and adore,
Honouring our Lord, forevermore.
Our lives, a testament to His gracious name,
Reflecting his Love, in this fleeting frame.

(XXXII)

"Lord, your ways surpass my understanding",
Author of my story, guiding my path unfolding,
I lean on you, trusting your divine plan,
Unveiling each chapter, minute by minute, hand in hand.

Your wisdom exceeds mine, in every test,
I surrender to your will, forever at rest,
Each Sunrise brings new pages to explore,
Eternity's narrative, crafted by your loving care.

In your hands, my future shines bright,
Secure in your promise, banishing endless night,
Through life's journey, I cling to your design,
Faithful author, writing beauty, line by line.

May every moment reflect your gracious Love,
As I trust your sovereignty, sent from above,
In your story, I find solace and peace,
Forever entwined, my heart releases.

(XXXIII)

God created Adam and Eve,
A perfect pair, in His divine plan to breathe,
Male and female, He made them with Love,
Complementing each other, sent from above.

In Eden's garden, they lived with glee,
Reflecting God's image and His glory,
Their bond was pure, their love so bright,
A beautiful Masterpiece in morning light.

Some may stray from God's original design,
But scripture stands, forever aligned,
Genesis speaks, of Adam and Eve,
A Biblical truth, of God's creative worth!

Respectful dialogue, we all can share,
Embracing diversity, with loving care,
Yet, Biblical truth remain our guiding light,
Adam and Eve, God's original delight.

(XXXIV)

In solitude, I find my peace,
A refuge from life's chaotic release,
Where thoughts align, and heart beats slow,
I hear God's whisper, "Wait and know."

In stillness, wisdom's lessons unfold,
Patience and calm, like treasures to hold,
No rush, no haste, just quiet trust,
God's command awaits like morning dust.

His voice, a whisper, gentle breeze,
Guiding steps, through life's complexities,
Solitude's silence, my soul revives,
In God's timing, my heart survives.

So I'll wait, in solitude's embrace,
Trusting His plan, His perfect pace,
For in stillness, I hear his voice clear,
Wait, my Child, my timing draws near.

(XXXV)

Words, whisper of the Heart,
Echoes that never depart,
Spoken, written or unspoken too,
They hold the power to see us through.

With gentle touch, they soothe the soul,
Comforting whispers that makes us whole,
Yet, with sharp edge, they cut like a knife,
Leaving scars that linger, a lifelong strife.

They dance upon the page, a wondrous spin,
Weaving tales that transport us within,
Ink-born messengers, they travel time and space,
Carrying dreams, hope and love's warm, tender pace.

Silent words, unspoken thoughts and hidden fears,
Linger within, through all our laughter and tears,
For words, though fleeting leave an indelible mark,
A testament to Love, Joy, Sorrow and the Human spark.

***May our words be WISE, KIND and TRUE,**
Reflecting the beauty that shines within me and you.